D1742681

PEGAN MEAL FOR

BEGINNERS

The Killer Pegan Meal Blueprint is here! Step by step Guide to Go Pegan for Beginners in Less than 24 Hours with Secrets Meal Preparation Tips that No One Wants to Share

© Copyright 2021 - All rights reserved.
The content contained within this book may not be reproduced, duplicated or transmitted without direct written permission from the author or the publisher. Under no circumstances will any blame or legal responsibility be held against the publisher, or author, for any damages, reparation, or monetary loss due to the information contained within this book. Either directly or indirectly.

Legal Notice:
This book is copyright protected. This book is only for personal use. You cannot amend, distribute, sell, use, quote or paraphrase any part, or the content within this book, without the consent of the author or publisher.

Disclaimer Notice:
Please note the information contained within this document is for educational and entertainment purposes only. All effort has been executed to present accurate, up to date, and reliable, complete information. No warranties of any kind are declared or implied. Readers acknowledge that the author is not engaging in the rendering of legal, financial, medical or professional advice. The content within this book has been derived from various sources. Please consult a licensed professional before attempting any techniques outlined in this book. By reading this document, the reader agrees that under no circumstances is the author responsible for any losses, direct or indirect, which are incurred as a result of the use of information contained within this document, including, but not limited to, errors, omissions, or inaccuracies.

Table of Contents

INTRODUCTION

Pegan diet involves both vegan and paleo. he essential nutritional category for the pegan diet is vegetables and organic product — these ought to include 75% of your all out consumption. Low-glycemic leafy foods, like berries and non-bland vegetables, ought to be stressed to limit your glucose reaction. Limited quantities of dull vegetables and sweet natural products might be took into consideration the individuals who have effectively accomplished solid glucose control preceding beginning the diet.

The pegan diet centers emphatically around entire food varieties, or food sources that have gone through next to zero handling before they make it to your plate.

Albeit most grains and vegetables are debilitate on the pegan diet because of their capability to impact glucose, some without gluten entire grains and vegetables are allowed in restricted amounts.

Grain admission ought not surpass in excess of a 1/2 cup (125 grams) per dinner, while vegetable admission ought not surpass 1 cup (75 grams) each day. Here are a few grains and vegetables that you may eat:

Grains: Black rice, quinoa, amaranth, millet, teff, oats

Vegetables: Lentils, chickpeas, dark beans, pinto beans

Pagan diet meals

40+ recipes

1. Shrimp Cobb Salad with Lemon Garlic Vinaigrette

Prep Time: 10 minutes Cook Time: 10 minutes Total Time: 20 minutes Servings: 6

INGREDIENTS:

- dressing:
- 2 tbsp new lemon juice
- 1 tsp fiery brown mustard
- 3 cloves garlic minced
- 1/8 tsp ocean salt
- 1/8 tsp dark pepper

- 1/4 cup olive oil (utilize one you like the kind of since it will come through!
- serving of mixed greens:
- 1 lb shrimp stripped and deveined
- Base sense of taste ocean depths preparing OR salt and pepper to prepare shrimp
- 1 tbsp natural coconut oil or delivered bacon fat to brush on barbecue or flame broil dish
- 6-8 cuts nitrate free bacon cooked and disintegrated (use sugar free for Whole30)
- 3 huge eggs delicate bubbled (see guidelines)
- 3/4 cup cherry tomatoes split
- 1 ready avocado
- 5 oz holder child spinach or your #1 serving of mied greens
- Daintily cut chives or scallions for decorate

DIRECTIONS:

1. dressing:
2. Spot all ingredients in a tall thin holder and mix with a drenching blender.
3. Then again, you can utilize a standard blender (or hand rush) to consolidate all ingredients EXCEPT the oil, and afterward gradually stream

in the oil while proceeding to mix. The consistency ought to be to some degree thick and the shading rich.

4. Have all ingredients all set (counting cooked and disintegrated bacon, prior to starting)
5. delicate heat up your eggs:
6. Carry a pot of water to bubbling and set up a bowl of ice water for after eggs cook. Cautiously lower each egg into water.
7. Bubble eggs 6 minutes, changing heat to keep water at a medium bubble.
8. Eliminate eggs each in turn with a spoon and spot in ice water for 2-3 minutes or until warm.
9. Cautiously strip eggs (I do this in the water, it appears to make it simpler!) and put to the side until prepared to serve.
10. flame broil shrimp:
11. Heat your flame broil or barbecue container to high heat and brush with coconut oil. Sprinkle shrimp done with base sense of taste preparing or salt and pepper.
12. Cook first side 2 minutes flip and keep on cooking another 2-3 minutes or until pink and obscure with brilliant brown.

13. gather plate of mixed greens:

14. Spot greens on the lower part of a serving bowl or platter, at that point mastermind the tomatoes, bacon, shrimp, and avocado (diced or cut) over the top. Cautiously cut each egg and orchestrate around plate of mixed greens. Throw with dressing preceding serving or serve dressing as an afterthought. Enjoy!

2. Cinnamon-Sweet Potatoes

INGREDIENTS: :

- 4-sweet potatoes
- Honey-cinnamon butter
- 2-cups butter softened
- ¼-cup of honey
- 2-tablespoons brown sugar
- 1-teaspoon ground cinnamon

DIRECTIONS::

1. Heat the oven to 375 ° F.
2. Wash and prick the sweet potatoes and wrap them in foil.
3. Bake the potatoes for an hour, or until completely soft.

4. Meanwhile, mix all the ingredients for the butter.

5. Cut the sweet potatoes open and use a fork to fluff the flesh. Add a dollop of butter to the steaming potato and serve.

6. Store leftover butter in the refrigerator.

3. Paleo Creamy Broccoli and Bacon Soup

(Ready in about 20 minutes | Servings 4)

INGREDIENTS: :

- Two slices bacon, chopped
- 2 tbsp scallions, chopped
- one carrot, chopped
- one celery, chopped
- salt, and black pepper, to taste
- one teaspoon garlic, finely chopped
- ½ teaspoon dried rosemary
- one sprig thyme, stripped and chopped
- ½ head green cabbage, shredded
- ½ head broccoli, broken into florets
- 3 cups water
- one mug of chicken stock
- ½ mug full-fat yogurt

DIRECTINS:

1. Heat a stockpot; now, sear the bacon until crisp: Reserve the bacon and one tablespoon of fat.

2. Then, cook scallions, carrots, and celery in 1 tablespoon of reserved fat. Put salt, pepper, and garlic; cook an extra 1 minute or until fragrant.

3. Now, mix in the rosemary, thyme, cabbage, and broccoli. Pour in water and stock, bringing to a rapid boil; lower flame and let it simmer for 10 minutes more.

4. Put yogurt and cook an extra 5 minutes, mixing occasionally. Use an immersion blender to puree your soup until smooth.

5. Taste and adjust the seasonings. Garnish with the cooked bacon just before serving.

4. Orange Spice Cheesecake (Dairy/Gluten/Sugar-Free)

Prep Time: 15 minutesTotal Time: 4 hours 15 minutes Servings: 10 Slices

INGREDIENTS:

- Hull
- 1 cup broiled almonds
- 1/2 cup broiled pepitas - or other nut/seed
- 2 Tbs coconut oil
- 1 Tbs monkfruit granules - or coconut sugar for non low-carb
- Touch of pink salt
- 1-2 Tbs water
- Cheesecake
- 1 cups whitened (skinless) almonds - splashed
- 1 cup crude cashews - doused
- 1/2 cup Lakanto maple syrup - or unadulterated maple syrup for non low-carb
- 1/2 cup coconut oil - dissolved

- Zing juice of 1 huge orange - 1/4 cup juice and + 1 Tbs zing
- 1/4 cup coconut cream
- 3/4 tsp cinnamon - to taste
- run of nutmeg, ginger or cloves - discretionary
- Touch of pink salt
- Enhancement
- Coconut whipped cream, orange cuts, orange zing and cinnamon

DIRECTIONS:

1. To make the covering:
2. Heartbeat together almonds and pepitas a couple of times in a food processor to separate. Include coconut oil, monkfruit and salt and mix again until a tacky batter structures, adding water toward the finish to help remain together.
3. Press into a 7" springform dish fixed with material. Freeze while you set up the filling.
4. To make the filling:
5. (Utilize nuts that have been absorbed boiling water for 2 hours least) Drain, flush and shake dry, at that point mix almonds and cashews in a food processor for in any event 5 minutes, until totally separated into a thick paste.
6. Add remaining ingredients and mix smooth.
7. Taste and adapt to season (more sugar, zing, flavor). Pour over covering.
8. Wrap with foil and freeze around 2 hours or until firm. Eliminate from springform and refrigerate until prepared to serve.

9. Embellish with whipped coconut cream (formula in takes note of) an orange cut and a cleaning of cinnamon. ENJOY

5.   Paleo Balsamic Zucchini Saute

Total Time Prep/Total Time: 20 min. Makes 4 servings

INGREDIENTS:
- 1 tablespoon olive oil
- 3 medium zucchini, cut into dainty cuts
- 1/2 cup chopped sweet onion
- 1/2 teaspoon salt
- 1/2 teaspoon dried rosemary, squashed
- 1/4 teaspoon pepper
- 2 tablespoons balsamic vinegar
- 1/3 cup disintegrated feta cheddar

DIRECTIONS:
1. In a large skillet, heat oil over medium-high heat; saute zucchini and onion until fresh delicate, 6-8 minutes. Mix in flavors. Add vinegar; cook and mix 2 minutes. Top with cheddar.

6. Low Carb Turkey And Peppers

PREP TIME: 20 MINUTES COOK TIME: 15 MINUTES
TOTAL TIME: 20 MINUTES YIELD: 4 SERVINGS

INGREDIENTS:

- 1 teaspoon salt, isolated
- 1 pound turkey tenderloin, cut into slight steaks about ¼-inch thick
- 2 tablespoons extra-virgin olive oil, isolated
- ½ large sweet onion, cut
- 1 red ringer pepper, cut into strips
- 1 yellow ringer pepper, cut into strips
- ½ teaspoon Italian flavoring
- ¼ teaspoon ground dark pepper
- 2 teaspoons red wine vinegar
- 1 14-ounce can squashed tomatoes, ideally fire-cooked
- Chopped new parsley and basil for decorate (optional)

Guidelines

1. Sprinkle ½ teaspoon salt over turkey. Heat 1 tablespoon oil in a large non-stick skillet over medium high heat. Add half of the turkey and cook, until browned on the last, 1 to 3 minutes. Flip and keep cooking until cooked completely through, 1 to 2 minutes. Eliminate the turkey to a plate with an opened spatula, tent with foil to keep warm. Add the excess 1 tablespoon oil to the skillet, diminish heat to medium and rehash with the leftover turkey, 1 to 3 minutes for every side.

2. Add onion, chime peppers and the leftover ½ teaspoon salt to the skillet, cover and cook, eliminating top to mix frequently, until the onion and peppers are relaxing and brown in spots, 5 to 7 minutes.

3. Eliminate top, increment heat to medium high, sprinkle with Italian flavoring and pepper and cook, blending regularly until the spices are fragrant, around 30 seconds. Add vinegar, and cook, mixing until totally dissipated, around 20 seconds. Add tomatoes and bring to a stew, blending regularly.

4. Add the turkey to the skillet with any amassed juices from the plate and bring to a stew. Diminish heat to medium-low and cook, turning in the sauce until the turkey is hot entirely through, 1 to 2 minutes. Serve finished off with parsley and basil if using.

7. Paleo Coconut Curry Pumpkin Soup

YIELDS:4 PREP TIME:0 HOURS 15 MINS TOTAL TIME:0 HOURS 30 MINS

INGREDIENTS: :
- 2 tbsp. extra-virgin olive oil
- 1 little onion, finely chopped
- 1 clove garlic, minced
- 2 tsp. new ginger, ground (or 1 tsp. ground ginger)
- 2 tsp. curry powder
- 1/2 tsp. cinnamon
- 1 tsp. nutmeg
- 1/2 tsp. cloves
- genuine salt
- Newly ground dark pepper
- 3 c. pumpkin puree (new or canned)
- 1/4 c. brown sugar, pressed
- 4 c. vegetable (or chicken) stock
- 1 14-oz. would coconut be able to drain
- Toasted pumpkin seeds, for decorate
- Cilantro leaves, for decorate

DIRECTIONS::

1. Heat oil in enormous pot over medium-high heat. Add onion and cook until delicate, 4 to 5 minutes. Add garlic and ginger, blending, until fragrant, 1 moment. Mix in curry, cinnamon, nutmeg, and cloves and season with salt and pepper.

2. Mix in pumpkin puree and brown sugar, at that point rush in vegetable stock and bring to bubble. Decrease heat and stew until marginally thickened, around 15 minutes. Add coconut milk, cooking over low heat, until warmed through, at that point season with salt and pepper.

3. Serve in bowls and topping with toasted pumpkin seeds and cilantro.

8. Smoky Cauliflower Bites

Total Time Prep/Total Time: 20 min. Makes 4 servings

INGREDIENTS:
- 3 tablespoons olive oil
- 3/4 teaspoon sea salt
- 1 teaspoon paprika
- 1/2 teaspoon ground cumin
- 1/4 teaspoon ground turmeric
- 1/8 teaspoon chili powder
- 1 medium head cauliflower, broken into florets

DIRECTIONS::
1. Firstly preheat oven to 450°. Mix first 6
2. Add cauliflower florets; toss to coat. Transfer to a 15x10x1-in. baking pan. Roast until tender, 15-20 minutes, stirring halfway.

9. Paleo White Sandwich

INGREDIENTS:

- 6-pasture eggs (try to get soy-free)
- 1/4 teaspoon of stevia powder extract or 2-tablespoons of honey
- 1/4 cup coconut oil, melted
- 1/2 teaspoon coconut vinegar (or apple cider vinegar)
- 1 cup of blanched almond flour
- 1/4 cup ground flax (make sure it's golden)
- 3 tbsp coconut flour, sifted
- 1-teaspoon of baking powder
- 1/2 teaspoon of sea salt

DIRECTIONS::

1. Preheat the oven to 350 ° F.
2. Line an 8 x 4 ″ loaf pan with a strip of parchment covering only the bottom of the pan, not the sides.
3. In a large bowl, beat the eggs, sweetener, coconut oil, and vinegar until well blended.
4. In a separate bowl, combine the almond flour, flax flour, coconut flour, baking powder, and sea salt until well blended.
5. Pour into the parchment-lined bread pan and bake for 35-40 minutes.

6. Remove from oven and let cool in the pan for 12 minutes.
7. Remove from pan by pulling up the parchment paper.
8. Place the bread on a wire rack to cool completely for 15 minutes.
9. Cut into slices and enjoy this paleo white sandwich bread recipe.
10. Keep it in the fridge for a week or a few months in the freezer

10. Paleo Cinnamon Swirls

Prep Time: 15 minutes Cooking Time: 30 minutes
Total Time: 45 minutes

INGREDIENTS:
- 4-eggs separated
- 1/4 teaspoon whipped cream
- 2 tbsp butter melted
- 2 tbsp butter softened
- 1-teaspoon of vanilla
- 3 oz cream cheese softened
- Liquid Stevia To Taste I used about 12 drops
- 1-teaspoon of baking powder
- 1 cup of almond flour
- 1 1/2 teaspoons of cinnamon divided
- 1/4 cup Erythritol I prefer confectioners

DIRECTIONS::
1. Preheat the oven to 350 degrees F and prepare a 9×5 " loaf pan with non-stick spray.
2. Divide the eggs between 2 large bowls.
3. Add the cream pie to the egg whites and beat with an electric mixer until soft peaks. Put aside.

4. Add softened butter, vanilla, cream cheese, and stevia to the egg yolks. Mix until well blended. Then add 1/2 teaspoon of cinnamon, baking powder, and almond flour and stir until well blended.
5. In a small bowl, combine the melted butter, erythritol, and the remaining one teaspoon of cinnamon. Stir to combine and set aside.
6. Fold the egg white into the egg yolk mixture. This can take a few minutes as the egg yolk mixture can be quite thick.
7. Pour half of the egg mixture into the prepared bread pan. Divide evenly with the cinnamon and butter mixture. Then the remaining egg mixture, making sure that the mixture is spread to the edges of the pan.
8. Make swirls in the bread with a butter knife and hold the knife vertically to avoid mixing too much between the layers.
9. Bake for 30-40 minutes or until the top is golden brown

11. Smoked Gouda Veggie Melt

Total Time Prep/Total Time: 25 min. Makes 4 servings

INGREDIENTS:

- 1 cup chopped fresh mushrooms
- 1 cup chopped fresh broccoli
- 1 medium sweet red pepper, chopped
- 1 small onion, chopped
- 2 tablespoons olive oil
- 8 slices Italian bread (1/2 inch thick)
- 1/2 cup mayonnaise
- 1 garlic clove, minced
- 1 cup shredded smoked Gouda cheese

DIRECTIONS::

1. Firstly preheat oven to 425°. Place mushrooms, broccoli, pepper and onion in a greased 15x10x1-in. baking pan. Drizzle with oil; toss to coat. Then roast 10-12 minutes or until tender.
2. Meanwhile, put bread slices on a baking sheet. Mix mayonnaise and garlic; spread over bread.
3. Change oven setting to broil. Spoon vegetables over bread slices; drizzle with cheese. Broil 3-4

in from heat 2-3 minutes or until cheese is melted.

12. Lemon Grass and Rice Noodle Soup

YIELD 4 servings TIME 1 hour

INGREDIENTS:
- 2 teaspoons crude nut oil or sesame oil
- 1 huge onion, in thick cuts
- 1 3-inch piece ginger, stripped and daintily cut
- ½ cup daintily cut lemon grass
- 1 2-inch piece cinnamon stick
- 2 star anise
- 4 cloves
- ½ teaspoon coriander seeds, squashed
- ½ teaspoon fennel seeds, squashed
- 4 little dry red chiles
- ⅛ teaspoon turmeric
- 2 teaspoons sugar
- 1 tablespoon soy sauce
- 2 teaspoons Asian fish sauce
- 8 cups fish stock or chicken stock
- Salt and pepper
- 8 ounces dainty rice noodles (vermicelli)
- 2 pounds mussels, scoured
- 1 pound squid, cut 1/2-inch thick
- ½ cup generally chopped cilantro, for embellish

- ¼ cup chopped scallions, for embellish
- Leaves from 1 little bundle Thai basil, for embellish
- 6 new green or red Thai bird chiles, fragmented, for decorate
- Lime wedges, for decorate

DIRECTIONS::

1. Spot a weighty lined soup pot over medium-high heat. Add the nut oil, and twirl to cover. At the point when oil is hot, add the onion and cook for 5 minutes, blending, until relaxed and delicately browned. Add all the aromatics (ginger, lemon grass, cinnamon, star anise, cloves, coriander, fennel, dry chiles and turmeric) and mix to circulate. Add the sugar and let everything fry delicately, until sugar starts to caramelize, around 2 minutes. Add the soy sauce, fish sauce and stock. Heat to the point of boiling, at that point decrease heat to a delicate stew. Cook for 30 minutes. Strain, disposing of solids. Season to taste with the salt and a liberal measure of pepper. (May be ready a few hours ahead.)
2. Drench the rice noodles: Put the rice vermicelli in an enormous bowl. Cover with bubbling water. Mix noodles as they mollify. Drench for around 20 minutes until delicate. Cool in a colander under running water and channel. Save at room temperature.
3. To serve, carry soup to a lively stew. Add the mussels and put on the cover. Cook 2 minutes, until mussels have opened. Add the squid, mix

to join and cook 30 seconds more. Mood killer heat.

4. Separation rice noodles among 4 enormous soup bowls. Spoon soup into bowls. Sprinkle with the cilantro, scallions and Thai basil. Pass the new chiles and lime wedges independently.

13. Paleo Healthy Garlic Bread

INGREDIENTS:
- 6-eggs separated
- 1-teaspoon of tartar
- 1/4 cup unflavored egg white protein powder (or 1/2 cup whey protein)
- 1-clove of garlic (or powder)

DIRECTIONS::
1. Separate the eggs and beat the egg whites with the tartar cream for a few minutes until VERY stiff. Very slowly, add whey protein (or egg white protein if dairy is sensitive). Fold the reserved yolks and herbs into the beaten egg whites. Grease a loaf pan very well. Spoon the mixture into the pan and smooth the top with a spatula. Select Low Carb program or Gluten Free one, and the select the size of the loaf.
2. Set the loaf size and the crust color for a preset menu.
3. Cool completely before cutting. Cut into 12 pieces. I also smear a little butter on each piece and rub it with garlic cloves (if not dairy sensitive, sprinkle with Parmesan cheese). I tossed it back in the bread machine for 3

minutes until the butter was fizzy and lightly browned.

14. Paleo Black Eyed Peas

Prep Time: 5 minutes Cook Time: 3 hours Servings: 4 Calories: 402kcal

INGREDIENTS:

- 15 ounces (3 cans) black-eyed-peas, un-drained
- pounds boneless pork chops
- 1 large onion, chopped
- salt and pepper to taste
- garlic powder to taste

DIRECTIONS::

1. Firstly Open and pour the three cans of black eyed peas into the slow cooker and season with salt and pepper to your taste.
2. Season both sides of the pork chops with salt, pepper, and garlic powder. Place in an even layer on top of the black eyed peas in the slow cooker.
3. Then Top the seasoned pork chops with the chopped onion in an even layer. Season with more salt and pepper to taste if you prefer.
4. Place the cover on the slow cooker and cook on low for 6 to 8 hours or on high for 2 to 4 hours

depending on your slow cooker. Remove the lid occasionally to stir.

5. Once the time is up, check the pork chops for the desired doneness. Now Serve over rice with a side of southern cornbread.

15. Crock Pot Baked Potatoes

Prep Time10 minutes Cook Time5 hours Total Time5 hours 10 minutes Servings 6

INGREDIENTS:

- 4-6 reddish brown potatoes
- 2-3 tsp olive oil 1/2 tsp per potato
- 1-1.5 tsp legitimate salt 1/4 tsp per potato
- aluminum foil
- margarine, cheddar, chives, bacon, acrid cream, salt and pepper

DIRECTIONS::

1. Wash and dry the potatoes, at that point utilize a fork to jab the potatoes all finished.
2. Spot every potato in the focal point of a piece of aluminum foil adequately huge to totally wrap the potato.
3. Rub all sides of every potato with 1/2 tsp olive oil and 1/4 tsp genuine salt.
4. Firmly fold the foil over the potatoes and spot them in a stewing pot.

5. Cook on High for 4-5 hours or Low for 8-10 hours until delicate. Be certain you don't overcook them.
6. Whenever they're done eliminate from the simmering pot and cautiously remove the foil.
7. Cut every potato down the middle the long way and top with your decision of margarine, cheddar, chives, bacon, acrid cream, salt and pepper, or some other most loved fixing. Appreciate!

16. Orleans Red Beans And Rice

Preparation Time : 10 min Serving :4

INGREDIENTS:

- 1 pound dry red beans, drenched for the time being (discretionary)
- 1 pound andouille wiener, cleaved
- 1 yellow onion, diced
- 1 green chime pepper, diced
- 2 celery stems, diced
- 5 cups water
- 1 tablespoon granulated onion
- 2 teaspoons granulated garlic
- 3 chicken bouillon 3D shapes
- 1 stick spread (8 tablespoons) cut (discretionary)
- The Boot preparing, to taste (or an elective Cajun preparing)
- rice, for serving
- salt, to taste (discretionary)

DIRECTIONS::

1. Earthy colored andouille wiener cuts in an enormous skillet over medium warmth. When cooked, eliminate andouille from skillet and put in a safe spot.
2. Add onion, green ringer pepper, and celery to a similar skillet. Sauté vegetables in hotdog drippings for 3 to 5 minutes or until delicate.
3. Shower within the slow cooker or pressing factor cooker pot a with non-stick cooking splash. Add red beans, andouille, onion, ringer pepper, celery, and water to the pot.
4. Mix in granulated onion, granulated garlic, and chicken bouillon 3D shapes.
5. Cover slow cooker or pressing factor cooker with top and Slow Cook on High for 4 hours.
6. Cautiously eliminate cover and mix in margarine and The Boot (or other Cajun preparing) to the pot.
7. Cover with top and keep cooking on High Pressure for hour.
8. Cautiously eliminate top.
9. Scoop red beans over rice and serve warm.

17. Paleo Cheesy Garlic Bread

INGREDIENTS:

- 170 g pre-sliced grated cheese mozzarella
- 85 g almond flour/flour
- 2 tbsp full cream cheese
- 1 tbsp crushed garlic
- 1 tbsp parsley, fresh or dried
- 1 tsp baking powder
- pinch of salt to taste
- 1-egg medium Metric grams

DIRECTIONS::

1. Turn on the bread machine. Mix all INGREDIENTS in bread machine pan and stir. Add the egg and mix gently to make a cheesy dough. Place them on a pan and shape them into a garlic bun. Cut slices into the low-carb garlic bread. Mix 2 tbsp melted butter, 1 tsp parsley, and 1 tsp garlic. Select Low Carb program, and the select the size of the loaf.
2. Brush the top of the low-carb garlic bread, sprinkle with more cheese

18. Flourless Cheese Pants

INGREDIENTS:
- FOR THE BREADSTICKS
- 1 1/2 cups shredded mozzarella cheese
- 2-large eggs
- 1/2 teaspoon of Italian seasoning
- BEFORE THE TOPPING
- 1/2 cup of grated mozzarella cheese
- 2 tbsp grated Parmesan cheese optional
- 1 tsp finely chopped parsley optional

DIRECTIONS::
1. Preheat the oven to 350 ° F. Line a 23 x 23 cm square baking pan with parchment paper. (I like to do the two sheets of parchment paper in the opposite
2. In a food processor, add 1 1/2 cups of cheese, eggs, and herbs. Mix until combined.
3. Spoon the batter into the baking tin. Gently distribute the mixture until it evenly covers the bottom of the pan. Place in the oven and bake for about 20 minutes. The crust should be fairly firm, with no wet dough remaining.

Remove from oven and let cool for a few minutes.

4. Preheat the oven to 425 ° F. Carefully remove the crust from parchment paper and place it on an oven-safe cooling rack. The cooling rack ensures that the bottom becomes crispy. Sprinkle the surface with the remaining 1/2 cup of cheese. If desired, you can replace two tablespoons of parmesan cheese with 2-tablespoons of mozzarella, giving it a slightly different flavor. Place the cooling rack in the oven and bake the breadsticks for about 5 minutes or until the cheese is melted and blistered.

5. If desired, sprinkle with parsley before cutting and serving.

19. Fathead Cheese Sticks

INGREDIENTS:

- 1 3/4 cups shredded mozzarella, I used an Italian blend for this dough; mozzarella is the most popular choice
- 3/4 cup of almond flour
- 2 tbsp cream cheese
- 1 The Happy Egg Co. egg
- Spices - garlic powder, Italian herbs, and my favorite addition for a kick is "Extra Spicy" salt-free Mrs. Dash

DIRECTIONS::

1. Preheat your oven to 425 *.
2. Start by mixing the grated cheese, cream cheese, and herbs in a microwave-safe bowl.
3. Microwave the cheese for 30 seconds, stir, and microwave again for one full minute. The mixture will get very hot, so be careful when moving the bowl.
4. Add the almond flour and mix gently.
5. Add the egg and mix gently. I use the back of a spoon or fork to "mash" everything together so that it blends well.

6. Once the dough is formed, place it on a large piece of parchment paper.
7. Place another sheet of parchment paper on top and roll out the dough with a rolling pin until it is thin and, if possible, a rectangle. The shape doesn't matter, but try to get it about 1/4 inch thick. Remove the top piece of parchment paper.
8. Place the dough and bottom layer of parchment paper on a baking tray and bake in the oven for about 10 minutes or until brown.
9. At this point, you can flip it over and bake for a few more minutes or continue.
10. Either way, sprinkle some more cheese on top and bake until the cheese is melted in just a few minutes.
11. Once you've let this cool, use a pizza cutter to cut into strips, small squares, or
12. Serve with a low-carb pizza sauce or marinara for dipping.

20. Avocado Cloud Bread

INGREDIENTS:

- 3-large eggs separated
- ¼ tsp onion powder
- ¼ tsp garlic powder
- ¼ teaspoon of tartar
- 3-tablespoons (about 39 grams) of mashed avocado must be mashed first before measuring
- 2 tsp sesame seeds

DIRECTIONS::

1. In a large bowl, add egg yolks, mashed avocado, onion powder, and garlic powder. Beat until evenly blended and smooth out as many small lumps of avocado as possible.
2. In a clean bowl of a food processor, add egg whites and tartar. Beat with a wire whisk at high speed until the egg whites become stiff peaks.
3. You can do both of the above steps in bread machine pan also.
4. Gently fold the egg white into the avocado mixture in 3 portions.

5. Spoon the full 1/4 cup of batter onto a baking sheet, about three inches apart. You should have enough batter for 12 rounds, 6 per sheet.
6. Plug in the bread machine and Select Low Carb program or Gluten Free one, and the select the size of the loaf.
7. Set the loaf size and the crust color for a preset menu or specify you own setting for the HOME MADE menu. Pour the batter into pan.
8. Bake for about 25-30 minutes or until the top and edges are golden brown.
9. Use a cookie spatula to remove bread from thepan. When they are done cooking, they should come off easily. If they are still attached, they will likely need a longer baking time.

21. Paleo Cheesy Broccoli Soup

Total Time Prep: 15 min. Cook: 3 hours Makes 4 servings

INGREDIENTS:

- 2 tablespoons spread
- 1 little onion, finely chopped
- 2 cups finely chopped new broccoli
- 3 cups decreased sodium chicken stock
- 1 can (12 ounces) dissipated milk
- 1/2 teaspoon pepper
- 1 bundle (8 ounces) measure cheddar (Velveeta), cubed
- 1-1/2 cups destroyed extra-sharp cheddar
- 1 cup destroyed Parmesan cheddar
- Extra destroyed extra-sharp cheddar

DIRECTIONS:

1. In a little skillet, heat spread over medium-high heat. Add onion; cook and mix 3-4 minutes or until delicate. Move to a 3-or 4-qt. slow cooker. Add broccoli, stock, milk and pepper.

2. Cook, covered, on low 3-4 hours or until broccoli is delicate. Mix in measure cheddar until dissolved. Add destroyed cheeses; mix until dissolved. Not long prior to serving, mix soup to join. Top servings with extra cheddar.

22. Paleo Loaded Slow-Cooker Potatoes

YIELDS:6 PREP TIME:0 HOURS 15 MINSNCOOK TIME:5 HOURS 0 MINS TOTAL TIME:5 HOURS 15 MINS

INGREDIENTS:

- Cooking shower
- 2 lb. infant potatoes, split and quartered assuming enormous
- 3 c. destroyed Cheddar
- 2 cloves garlic, meagerly cut
- 8 cuts bacon, cooked
- 1/4 c. cut green onions, in addition to additional for decorate
- 1 tbsp. paprika
- legitimate salt
- Newly ground dark pepper
- Sharp cream, sprinkling

DIRECTIONS::

1. Line a slow cooker with foil and splash with cooking shower. Add a large portion of the potatoes, 1/4 cups cheddar, a large portion of the garlic, 1/3 of the cooked bacon, a large portion of the green onions, and a large portion of the paprika. Season with salt and pepper. Rehash.

2. Cover and cook on high until potatoes are delicate, 5 to 6 hours. (The greater your potatoes, the more they'll require.) About 20 to 30 minutes prior to serving, top with residual cheddar and bacon (this is your second to make the potatoes look pretty!)

3. Embellishment with more green onions and sprinkle with sharp cream prior to serving.

23. Sweet Potato Souffle

Serves: 8 servings Prep time: 30 minutes Cook time: 1 hour Total time: 1 hr 30 min

INGREDIENTS:
- 3-4 pounds yams (stripped and cubed)
- 1 stick (1/2 cup) unsalted spread (liquefied + 3 tablespoons)
- 3 huge eggs (daintily beaten)
- 1/2 cup light brown sugar
- 1 cup cream (or entire milk)
- 1/2 cup self-rising flour (or better self rising cake flour)
- 1 teaspoon vanilla concentrate
- 1/2 teaspoon salt
- 1 cup chopped walnuts (broiled)
- Cinnamon Sugar:
- 1/4 cup white sugar (or light brown sugar)
- 1/2 teaspoon ground cinnamon
- 1/4 cup unsalted spread (liquefied)

DIRECTIONS:

1. Preheat oven to 350 degrees F. Orchestrate the oven rack in the oven.
2. Margarine or splash with heating shower a 9x13 inch meal or preparing dish. Put in a safe spot.
3. Add 1 cup of walnuts to a heating sheet and dish for a couple of moments. Watch near not consume them. Eliminate from oven, cool and generally cleave.
4. Cook Sweet Potatoes:
5. Meanwhile, add the cubed potatoes to a dutch oven or enormous sauce dish. Cover with water and sprinkle some salt, heat to the point of boiling. Bubble for around 15 minutes, when punctured with a fork, the potatoes ought to be delicate.
6. Channel cooked yams, pound until smooth and put to the side to chill a piece.
7. Cinnamon Sugar:
8. Consolidate the sugar and cinnamon in a little bowl. Mix and put in a safe spot.
9. Plan Souffle:
10. In a medium bowl consolidate: liquefied spread, brown sugar, beaten eggs, cream, vanilla, salt and flour. Whisk well to join, a hand blender can be utilized also.
11. Add the combination to the crushed yams and mix until very much consolidated. A hand blender can be utilized for this too.
12. Move the combination to the readied heating dish. Smooth the top.

13. Sprinkle with chopped walnuts and cinnamon sugar uniformly. Shower the excess 3 tablespoons of dissolved margarine on top.
14. Heat:
15. Cover dish with foil, to maintain a strategic distance from walnut beating from consuming. Heat for around 30 minutes, reveal and prepare for another 20-30 minutes or until puffed and delicately browned on the edges and top.
16. Serve quickly or cool and refrigerate for some other time.

24. Quinoa California Salad

INGREDIENTS:

- 1/2 cup of quinoa dry
- 1 cup of water for cooking quinoa
- 1-large mango cut into small pieces
- 1/4 small red onion chopped
- 1/2 red pepper chopped
- 3/4 cup grated coconut, unsweetened
- 3/4 cup almond slices or strips, toasted if desired
- 1 cup of raisins
- 1 cup edamame shelled, thawed if frozen
- 1/4 cup cilantro chopped, or parsley if you don't like cilantro

DIRECTIONS:

1. Cook the quinoa according to the directions on the package. Let cool.
2. Beat all the dressing INGREDIENTS together in a small bowl.
3. Toss all the salad INGREDIENTS along with the cooled quinoa in a large bowl and upload the dressing. Toss it tasty and serve cold.

25. Paleo Pumpkin Casserole

INGREDIENTS:
- 5-pounds of sweet potatoes
- 4-tablespoons of butter
- 2-eggs lightly beaten
- 1-teaspoon of salt
- 1-teaspoon of cinnamon powder
- 1/2 teaspoon vanilla extract
- 1/2 teaspoon nutmeg
- 1/2 cup of dark brown sugar
- 1/4 cup whipped cream
- Nonstick cooking spray
- 1/2 cup all-purpose flour
- 1 cup of dark brown sugar
- 1/4 teaspoon of salt
- 1 cup of quick-cooking oats
- 1/2 teaspoon of cinnamon powder
- 1/4 pound of butter
- 2 cups of miniature marshmallows

DIRECTIONS:

1. Preheat the oven to 350 degrees F.
2. Wrap sweet potatoes in foil, place on a baking tray, and bake for about 1 hour. After 1 hour, check if you are using a piercing with a fork; if you can pierce them quickly, they are done baking. If not, cook them a little longer and check again. Let the sweet potatoes cool until you can handle them, remove the foil and peel them off by pushing the pulp's surfaces.
3. Place the boiled potatoes in a large bowl. If you're using canned views, skip the trick. Just open the options and get out of the folder. Blend the candy potatoes with the butter using a pastry blender or potato masher until mostly clean.
4. Add the INGREDIENTS salt, flavor, vanilla and nutmeg and beat until you have a uniform mixture. Add the brown sugar and cream and mix well.
5. In a medium bowl, combine the flour, brown sugar, salt, something else, and cinnamon and stir well. Continue in the 1/4 pound butter with fat until you have a crumb mixture. If you had ever turned it off, heat it one more time to 350 levels F. Lightly brush a 9 x 13-inch baking pan with cooking spray.
6. I spread the candy potatoes in the pan. Cover with the marshmallows and drop the oatmeal crust at the marshmallows' peak - bake for 30 to forty-five minutes.

26. Pepper Sausage Pizza

Total Time Prep: 30 min. Bake: 20 min. Makes 15 slices

INGREDIENTS:

- 3 to 4 cups all-purpose flour, isolated
- 1 bundle (1/4 ounce) snappy ascent yeast
- 1 teaspoon sugar
- 1 cup warm water (120° to 130°)
- 1/4 cup olive oil
- 2 teaspoons salt
- 1 teaspoon dried basil
- 1/2 teaspoon pepper
- 1/2 cup shredded Parmesan cheddar, isolated
- 3 cups torn new spinach
- 1 can (15 ounces) pizza sauce
- 4 cups shredded mozzarella cheddar, isolated
- 1/2 pound mass pork frankfurter, cooked and depleted
- 1 medium onion, chopped
- 1/2 pound new mushrooms, cut
- 1/2 medium sweet yellow pepper, chopped
- 1-1/2 teaspoons pizza preparing or Italian flavoring
- 3 tablespoons minced new basil, optional

DIRECTIONS:

1. Preheat oven to 450°. In a bowl, join 1 cup flour, yeast and sugar. Add water; beat until smooth. Add the oil, salt, dried basil, pepper, 1/4 cup Parmesan cheddar and 2 cups flour; beat until mixed. Mix in sufficient excess flour to frame a delicate mixture. Turn onto a floured surface; ply until smooth and flexible, around 6-8 minutes. Cover and let rest 5 minutes.

2. In the mean time, place spinach in a microwave-safe bowl; cover and microwave on high 30 seconds or just until shriveled. Reveal and put in a safe spot.

3. Press mixture into a lubed 15x10x1-in. heating dish. Spread with pizza sauce; sprinkle with 2-1/2 cups mozzarella cheddar, wiener, onion, spinach, mushrooms and yellow pepper. Top with outstanding Parmesan and mozzarella cheeses. Sprinkle with pizza preparing. Heat 20 minutes or until outside layer is brilliant brown. Sprinkle with new basil whenever wanted. Cut into squares.

27. Spicy Roasted Sausage, Potatoes and Peppers

Total Time Prep: 20 min. Bake: 30 min. Makes 4 servings

INGREDIENTS:

- 1 pound potatoes (about 2 medium), peeled and cut into 1/2-inch cubes
- 1 package (12 ounces) fully cooked andouille chicken sausage links or flavor of your choice, cut into 1-inch pieces
- 1 medium red onion, cut into wedges
- 1 medium sweet red pepper, cut into 1-inch pieces
- 1 medium green pepper, cut into 1-inch pieces
- 1/2 cup pickled pepper rings
- 1 tablespoon olive oil
- 1/2 to 1 teaspoon Creole seasoning
- 1/4 teaspoon pepper

DIRECTIONS:

1. Firstly preheat oven to 400°. In a large bowl, combine potatoes, sausage, onion, red pepper, green pepper and pepper rings. Mix oil, Creole seasoning and pepper; drizzle over potato mixture and toss to coat.
2. Then transfer to a 15x10x1-in. baking pan coated with cooking spray. Roast until vegetables are tender, stirring occasionally, 30-35 minutes.

28. Paleo Curry-Roasted Turkey and Potatoes

Total Time Prep/Total Time: 30 min. Makes 4 servings

INGREDIENTS:
- 1 pound Yukon Gold potatoes (around 3 medium), cut into 1/2-inch solid shapes
- 2 medium leeks (white segment just), meagerly cut
- 2 tablespoons canola oil, isolated
- 1/2 teaspoon pepper, isolated
- 1/4 teaspoon salt, isolated
- 3 tablespoons Dijon mustard
- 3 tablespoons nectar
- 3/4 teaspoon curry powder
- 1 bundle (17.6 ounces) turkey bosom cutlets
- Minced new cilantro or meagerly cut green onions, optional

DIRECTIONS:

1. Preheat oven to 450°. Spot potatoes and leeks in a 15x10x1-in. heating dish covered with cooking splash. Shower with 1 tablespoon oil; sprinkle with 1/4 teaspoon pepper and 1/8 teaspoon salt. Mix to cover. Broil 15 minutes, mixing once.
2. Then, in a small bowl, consolidate mustard, nectar, curry powder and remaining oil. Sprinkle turkey with staying salt and pepper.
3. Sprinkle 2 tablespoons mustard blend over potatoes; mix to cover. Spot turkey over potato combination; shower with residual mustard blend. Broil 6-8 minutes longer or until turkey is not, at this point pink and potatoes are delicate. Whenever wanted, sprinkle with cilantro.

29. Vegan Southern Soul Bowl

Prep: 10 minsCook: 20 minsTotal: 30 mins Servings: 4 people

INGREDIENTS:

- Cornbread:
- cornbread formula here, prep early for ease
- Collards:
- 1 tbsp olive oil, additional virgin
- 4 cups collard greens, chopped – around one pack
- 2 cloves garlic, chopped
- 1-2 tbsp apple juice vinegar
- salt and pepper to taste
- Bar-b-que Tofu:
- 10 oz tofu, firm – cubed
- 1 cup veggie lover grill sauce, DIY or packaged (formula in notes)
- Messy Sauce:
- 3/4 cup yam, prepared – crushed – skin eliminated — 1 little potato
- 4-5 Tbsp veggie lover spread
- 1-2 cloves garlic
- 1/3 cup healthful yeast
- 1/2 cup pasta water, + add more to mix if necessary

- 1 Tbsp Dijon mustard
- 1/4 tsp salt
- 1/8 tsp turmeric, for shading – discretionary
- 1/4 cup veggie lover cheddar shreds, discretionary
- Other:
- 3 cups pasta shells

DIRECTIONS:
1. Cornbread
2. For ease, I instruct making the cornbread ahead concerning time if conceivable. This way you can simply get and cut. You can utilize a simple veggie lover blend, or follow the formula connected in notes.
3. Bar-b-que Tofu
4. Preheat oven to 375 and fix a heating sheet with material paper.
5. In a huge blending bowl, throw the tofu blocks with the bar-b-que sauce. at that point move the shapes and sauce to the preparing sheet. Spread in a far layer, so the shapes don't cover or cover one another.
6. Prepare at 375 for 15-20 minutes. Mood killer heat and let tofu rest for a couple of moments prior to serving.
7. Messy Shells
8. Heat an enormous pot of water to the point of boiling and add pasta shells. Cook until delicate – make sauce while bubbling.
9. Microwave your yam for 5-7 minutes, or until delicate. Eliminate skin. Crush and measure

out around 3/4 cups. You can serve any extra as another side dish.

10. Add all the messy sauce INGREDIENTS to a blender and mix from low to high until smooth.

11. Channel pasta and pour the greater part of the messy sauce up and over the pasta. Mix to consolidate and cushion. Put to the side in a warm pot with a top on.

12. Collards

13. You can begin your collards while your pasta is bubbling – since they just require a couple of moments. Add your olive oil and garlic to a skillet over high heat. At the point when oil is hot, include the collards. Throw a piece with the oil and garlic. At that point turn off heat and cover the collards with a top – even a weighty top will work. Allow them to sit for five minutes, at that point add the juice vinegar and salt and pepper – throw to consolidate – they ought to be pleasantly shriveled now.

14. Amass Plate

15. Add the tofu, collards, messy pasta and cornbread to each plate and serve!

16. Gear huge soup pot blender skillet preparing sheetmblending bowl cornbread dish

30. Paleo Bagels Recipe

INGREDIENTS:

- 2-teaspoons of dried yeast
- 1-teaspoon of inulin
- 2-tablespoons of warm water
- 10 ounces of mozzarella shredded
- 2-tablespoons of butter melted
- 6 ounces of almond flour
- 2-teaspoons of baking powder
- 1-teaspoon of xanthan gum
- 3-large eggs one is for egg washing
- 2-tablespoons of everything season

DIRECTIONS:

1. In a large mixing bowl, add the yeast, inulin, and warm water and set aside to rise. Melt the mozzarella and butter until completely melted. This can be done in the microwave or a saucepan on the stove. When the yeast is frothy, add the almond flour, baking powder, and xanthan gum and mix well. Pour over the hot melted cheese mixture and toss into the almond flour mixture; about halfway through the mix, add 2 of the eggs.

2. Keep mixing until you have a slightly sticky dough. I highly recommend mixing the dough with gloved hands for the best results. Set the dough aside and make a large baking tray by lining it with parchment paper.
3. Set your oven to 180C / 355F. Divide your dough into eight pieces of equal size. Ours weighed between 75-80g / 2.6-2.8oz. Roll each piece of dough into a ball and run your finger through the center to make an opening.
4. To make the opening wider, gently twist the dough around your finger as if it were a small hula hoop. Place your bagel on the parchment-lined baking sheet and repeat Step 8 for the remaining dough pieces.
5. Break the extra egg into a small bowl and beat well. Divide your Everything Seasoning on a plate ready for dipping.
6. Gently brush each bagel with an egg wash, then press them into the spices.
7. Return it to the baking sheet and move on to the other bagel. When all the bagels are seasoned, let them stand in a warm place for 15 minutes to rise.
8. Bake in the oven for 15-20 minutes, until brown. Remove from oven and let cool 10 minutes before enjoying.

31. Paleo Zucchini-Crusted Pizza

*Total Time Prep: 20 min. Bake: 25 min.
Makes 6 servings*

INGREDIENTS:

- 2 large eggs, gently beaten
- 2 cups shredded zucchini (around 1-1/2 medium), pressed dry
- 1/2 cup shredded part-skim mozzarella cheddar
- 1/2 cup ground Parmesan cheddar
- 1/4 cup universally handy flour
- 1 tablespoon olive oil
- 1 tablespoon minced new basil
- 1 teaspoon minced new thyme
- Fixings:
- 1 container (12 ounces) broiled sweet red peppers, julienned
- 1 cup shredded part-skim mozzarella cheddar
- 1/2 cup cut turkey pepperoni

DIRECTIONS:

1. Preheat oven to 450°. Blend the initial 8 INGREDIENTS move to a 12-in. pizza container covered liberally with cooking splash. Spread combination to a 11-in. circle.

2. Heat until light brilliant brown, 13-16 minutes. Lessen oven setting to 400°. Add garnishes. Prepare until cheddar is dissolved, 10-12 minutes longer.

32. Saucy Thai Butternut Squash Curry

prep time 15 minutes cook time 5 hours total time 5 hours 15 minutes servings 6 calories 382 kcal

INGREDIENTS:

- 1/3 cup Thai Red curry paste
- 2 jars (14 ounce) coconut milk
- 1-2 cups low sodium veggie stock
- 1 tablespoon fish sauce
- 1 tablespoon rich peanut butter
- 4 cups cubed butternut squash
- 1 stick cinnamon
- 1 inch new ginger, ground
- juice from 1 lime
- 2 cups destroyed kale
- 1 pound wide egg noodles, like tagliatelle
- 1/4 cup new cilantro, or basil, generally cleaved
- 1 pomegranate, arils for serving

DIRECTIONS:

1. In the bowl of your slow cooker, join together the curry paste, coconut milk, 1 cup stock, fish sauce, and peanut butter. Add the butternut squash, cinnamon, ginger, and lime juice. Season gently with salt and pepper. Cover and cook on low for 4-5 hours or on high for 2-3 hours.
2. Mix the kale into the curry and cook 5 minutes until shriveled. Mix in the cilantro (or basil). On the off chance that the curry is excessively thick, add stock to thin.
3. In the meantime, heat a huge pot of salted water to the point of boiling. Heat up the noodles as per bundle directions:.
4. To serve, split the noodles between bowls and spoon the curry up and over. Top with pomegranate arils and cilantro. Enjoy!
5. In the bowl of your moment pot, consolidate together the curry paste, coconut milk, 1 cup stock, fish sauce, and peanut butter. Add the butternut squash, cinnamon, ginger, and lime juice. Season daintily with salt and pepper. Cover, select the manual setting, and cook on high pressing factor for 8 minutes.
6. When done cooking, utilize the fast delivery capacity and delivery the steam. Set the moment pot to sauté. Mix in the kale and cook 5 minutes until shriveled. Mix in the cilantro (or basil). On the off chance that the curry is excessively thick, add stock to thin.

7. To serve, split the noodles between bowls and spoon the curry up and over. Top with pomegranate arils and cilantro. Enjoy!

33. Sausage and Pepper Sheet-Pan Sandwiches

Total Time Prep: 20 min. Bake: 30 min. Makes 6 servings

INGREDIENTS:

- 1 pound uncooked sweet Italian turkey hotdog joins, generally chopped
- 3 medium sweet red peppers, cultivated and cut
- 1 huge onion, split and cut
- 1 tablespoon olive oil
- 6 sausage buns, split
- 6 cuts provolone cheddar

DIRECTIONS:

1. Preheat oven to 375°. Spot wiener pieces in a 15x10x1-in. sheet skillet, orchestrating peppers and onion around frankfurter. Shower olive oil over wiener and vegetables; heat, mixing blend following 15 minutes, until frankfurter is not, at this point pink and vegetables are delicate, 30-35 minutes.
2. During the most recent 5 minutes of preparing, orchestrate buns cut side up in a subsequent sheet container; top every bun base with a

cheddar cut. Prepare until buns are brilliant brown and cheddar is softened.Spoon frankfurter and pepper combination onto bun bottoms. Supplant tops.

3. Extra pasta sauce in the cooler is an invite expansion for a pizza sandwich.
4. For a family-sized sandwich, trade out the wiener buns with an enormous portion of French bread cut down the middle longwise.

34. Asparagus-Mushroom Frittata

Total Time Prep: 25 min. Bake: 20 min. Makes 8 servings

INGREDIENTS:

- 8 large eggs
- 1/2 cup entire milk ricotta cheddar
- 2 tablespoons lemon juice
- 1/2 teaspoon salt
- 1/4 teaspoon pepper
- 1 tablespoon olive oil
- 1 bundle (8 ounces) frozen asparagus lances, defrosted
- 1 large onion, divided and daintily cut
- 1/2 cup finely chopped sweet red or green pepper
- 1/4 cup cut infant portobello mushrooms

DIRECTIONS:

1. Preheat oven to 350°. In a large bowl, whisk eggs, ricotta cheddar, lemon squeeze, salt and pepper. In a 10-in. ovenproof skillet, heat oil over medium heat. Add asparagus, onion, red pepper and mushrooms; cook and mix 6-8 minutes or until onion and pepper are delicate.
2. Eliminate from heat; eliminate asparagus from skillet. Hold eight lances; cut leftover asparagus into 2-in. pieces. Return slice asparagus to skillet; mix in egg combination. Organize held asparagus lances over eggs to take after spokes of a wheel.
3. Heat, revealed, 20-25 minutes or until eggs are totally set. Let stand 5 minutes. Cut into wedges.

35. Easy Paleo Cheese Broccoli

INGREDIENTS: :

- 2-tablespoons butter
- 2-tablespoons flour
- 1-cup whipped cream
- ½-cup milk
- ¼-teaspoon salt
- ¼-teaspoon black pepper
- ½-teaspoon paprika powder
- ¼-teaspoon cayenne powder
- ½-teaspoon garlic powder
- ½-teaspoon ground mustard
- 8-ounces crisp cheddar cheese, shredded (plus more for topping)
- 6–8 cups fresh broccoli florets, rinsed

DIRECTIONS: :
1. Preheat the oven to 375 ° F and coat 6 (10-ounces or so) casseroles with cooking spray.
2. Melt the butter in a large, heavy-bottomed pan or a Dutch oven. Beat in the flour. Cook and stir until the roux turns a light golden color.
3. Gradually beat in the cream and milk until smooth. Add the spices.

4. Cook over medium heat until the sauce thickens. Stir in cheese until melted.
5. Meanwhile, steam the broccoli in a separate pan until bright green but still crispy.
6. Add the broccoli to the white sauce and stir to coat.
7. Spoon the broccoli and white sauce into the prepared dishes. Top with more cheese.
8. Bake for 3-5 minutes, until the cheese melts on top and the edges are hot and bubbly.

36. Paleo White Pizza with Roasted Tomatoes

*Total Time Prep: 45 min. + roasting Bake: 25 min.
Makes 8 servings*

INGREDIENTS:

- 4 plum tomatoes (around 1 pound), cut longwise into 1/2-inch cuts and cultivated
- 1/4 cup olive oil
- 1 teaspoon sugar
- 1/2 teaspoon salt

Outside:
- 2 tablespoons olive oil
- 1 huge onion, finely chopped (around 1 cup)
- 2 teaspoons dried basil
- 2 teaspoons dried thyme
- 1 teaspoon dried rosemary, squashed
- 1 bundle (1/4 ounce) dynamic dry yeast
- 1 cup warm water (110° to 115°)
- 5 tablespoons sugar
- 1/4 cup olive oil
- 1-1/2 teaspoons salt
- 3-1/4 to 3-3/4 cups all-purpose flour

Topping:
- 1 cup entire milk ricotta cheddar
- 3 garlic cloves, minced
- 1/2 teaspoon salt
- 1/2 teaspoon Italian flavoring
- 2 cups shredded part-skim mozzarella cheddar

DIRECTIONS:

1. Preheat oven to 250°. In a bowl, throw tomatoes with oil, sugar and salt. Move to a lubed 15x10x1-in. heating container. Broil 2 hours or until tomatoes are delicate and somewhat withered.
2. For outside, in an enormous skillet, heat oil over medium-high heat. Add onion; cook and mix 3-4 minutes or until delicate. Mix in spices. Cool somewhat.
3. In a small bowl, break down yeast in warm water. In a huge bowl, join sugar, oil, salt, yeast combination and 1 cup flour; beat on medium speed until smooth. Mix in onion combination and enough leftover flour to shape a delicate mixture (batter will be tacky).
4. Turn batter onto a floured surface; massage until smooth and versatile, around 6-8 minutes. Spot in a lubed bowl, going once to oil the top. Cover with cling wrap and let ascend in a warm spot until practically multiplied, around 1-1/2 hours.
5. Preheat oven to 400°. Oil a 15x10x1-in. preparing container. Punch down batter; move to fit base and 1/2-in. up sides of container. Cover; let rest 10 minutes. Heat 10-12 minutes or until edges are daintily browned.

6. In a small bowl, blend ricotta cheddar, garlic, salt and Italian flavoring. Spread over covering; top with cooked tomatoes and mozzarella cheddar. Heat 12-15 minutes or until covering is brilliant and cheddar is liquefied.

37. Mediterranean Cauliflower Rice

Prep time: 30 min Cook time: min Servings: 3

WHAT YOU NEED

- 1 medium cauliflower, around 3 cups riced
- 1 tablespoon olive oil
- 1/4 cup onion, chopped
- 2 cloves garlic, minced
- 1 tablespoon lemon juice, about a large portion of a lemon crushed
- zing from a large portion of a lemon
- 2 tablespoons pinenuts
- 1/4 teaspoon red bean stew chips
- new parsley, chopped

HOW YOU MAKE IT

1. To start with, eliminate the cauliflower leaves and stems. Then, cleave it into reduced down florets. At that point drive the cauliflower into a running food processor using the grinding connection.
2. Second, heat the olive oil in a profound skillet using medium heat. Then, add the onion and

saute for around four to five minutes until it turns out to be delicate and clear. At that point, add the garlic and saute for another 1 to 2 minutes.

3. Third, raise the heat to high and add the cauliflower, lemon, zing, pine nuts, and stew drops. At that point, saute everything for about a moment. In any case, focus as you would prefer not to cook it to the point the cauliflower turns out to be excessively soft.

4. Fourth, eliminate from heat and mix in the parsley. At that point, season with salt and pepper to taste and serve.

38. Warm Brussels Sprout, Bacon and Spinach Salad

Prep time: 20 min Cook time: 5 min Servings: 3

WHAT YOU NEED

- 8 cuts bacon
- 2 cups Brussels sprouts, managed and meagerly cut
- 1/2 teaspoons caraway seed
- 3 tablespoons olive oil
- 3 tablespoons wine vinegar
- 1/4 teaspoon white sugar
- 1/2 pound spinach, chopped

HOW YOU MAKE IT

1. To start with, place the bacon in a profound skillet and cook over medium heat until brown. Then, disintegrate and put in a safe spot. At that point, steam the Brussels sprouts until delicate in a medium pan.

2. Second, heat the excess bacon fat. Then, add the Brussels fledglings and caraway seeds. At that point, saute everything for around one to two minutes until the Brussels sprouts are delicate.
3. Third, add the oil, vinegar, and sugar to the skillet and mix. Then, add the spinach and saute the blend for one to two minutes over medium heat until the spinach withers.
4. Fourth, season the plate of mixed greens with pepper and sprinkle with bacon. At that point, serve the plate of mixed greens warm as a side dish.

39. Toasted Coconut Chia Pudding

Prep time: 30 min Servings: 2

WHAT YOU NEED

- 1 cup unsweetened plain almond milk
- 1 cup coconut milk
- 1 teaspoon lime juice
- 2 tablespoons maple syrup
- 1/3 cup chia seeds
- 1 squeeze ocean salt
- 1/3 cup chia seeds
- 1/3 cup unsweetened shredded coconut
- 2 cups cubed tropical organic product (mango, pineapple, and so on)

HOW YOU MAKE IT

1. To start with, whisk together the coconut milk, maple syrup, lime juice, vanilla concentrate, and ocean salt. Then, add the chia seeds and rush for an extra one to two minutes. At that point, rest at room temperature for around 20 minutes, whisking at times.
2. Second, refrigerate the pudding for in any event three hours. Notwithstanding, chilling it short-term works best.

3. Third, add the coconut to an enormous non-stick skillet and toast over medium heat for around one to two minutes until light brown.
4. Fourth, mix the pudding and add to single-serving estimated bowls, Then, top with the cubed tropical leafy foods coconut. Serve right away.

40. Pegan Almond Milk

Prep time: 20 min Servings: 1

INGREDIENTS
- 4 cups water, separated
- 1 cup of almonds, doused for the time being
- 2 dates, pitted
- 1 teaspoon vanilla concentrate

HOW YOU MAKE IT
1. To start with, add the to a fast blender and mix until smooth.
2. Second, empty the fluid into a nut milk pack or piece of cheesecloth to channel.
3. Third, move the almond milk to a glass container or pitcher and refrigerate for a few hours prior to serving.
4. In the first place, Nut milk packs are somewhat of a knick knack and can be somewhat expensive. Therefore, I like to utilize paint skimming packs which can be bought at your neighborhood equipment or paint store.
5. Last, you can substitute different nuts like cashews for the almonds.

41. Paleo Baked Potato

INGREDIENTS: :
- 4-medium russet potatoes
- 4–6 tablespoons vegetable oil
- 1½-tablespoon kosher salt
- Optional: sour cream and chives for serving

DIRECTIONS::
1. Preheat the oven to 375 ° F.
2. Scrub and dry the potatoes and pierce them once or twice with a fork.
3. Rub oil all over the outside of the potatoes with clean hands. Sprinkle generously with salt.
4. Bake for 50 minutes and pick one with a fork. When it is cooked inside, the potatoes are done. If it still feels hard, put them back in the oven to cook a little longer.

42. Paleo Cheese & Bacon Rolls Recipe

INGREDIENTS: :

- 5 ounces Bacon diced
- 2-tablespoons of cream cheese
- 2-tablespoons of sesame seeds
- 1-tablespoon of Psyllium Husk
- 1 1/2 teaspoons baking powder
- 1 cup of cheddar cheese shredded
- 1/2 cup mozzarella cheese shredded
- 3-large eggs
- 1/2 teaspoon ground pepper
- 1-pinch of salt

DIRECTIONS:

1. Preheat the oven to 180C / 355F. Fry the bacon cubes in a skillet over medium heat until just starting to brown. Turn off the heat. Add the cream cheese to the Bacon and let it soften while the Bacon cools for 5 minutes. Put the Bacon and cream cheese mixture in your food processor, along with all other Reserve a spoonful of Bacon to cover the buns.

2. Blend on medium speed for 3-5 minutes until all are well combined. Spoon the mixture into 12 equal stacks on baking trays lined with parchment paper.
3. Sprinkle each sandwich with the reserved Bacon. Bake for 13-16 minutes until the buns are golden and puffy. Enjoy them warm from the oven or keep them in the fridge. They can be quickly reheated in a microwave or toaster.

43. Paleo Pumpkin Muffins

Preparation Time: 14-Mins | Cooking Time: 5-Mins | Serving: 5

INGREDIENTS:

- 1 1/2 cups of flour
- 3/4 cup sugar
- 1 tsp baking powder
- 1-teaspoon of baking powder
- 1/4 teaspoon of salt
- 1-teaspoon pumpkin pie spice
- 1 1/2 cups pumpkin puree
- 1/4 cup butter, melted/cooled
- 1-teaspoon of vanilla extract
- 1-egg
- 4 oz cream cheese, softened
- 1/2 teaspoon vanilla extract
- 1-teaspoon of flour
- 2 tbsp sugar
- 1-teaspoon of milk

DIRECTIONS:

1. Preheat the oven to 350 stages and line a muffin tray with liners or cooking spray.
2. In a large bowl, add the flour, sugar, baking powder, baking powder, salt, and pumpkin spice.
2. Place pumpkin, melted butter, vanilla extract, and egg in a separate bowl
3. Combine the wet mixture with the dry aggregate and stir until simply combined.
4. Fill muffin liners with batter about three / four full.
5. To make cream cheese filling: Put all substances in a bowl and integrate.
6. Using a play bag or layer with a different tip out and a dollop, what can you put in the muffin cups. It will sink almost completely.
7. Place the muffin tray in an oven to bake for about 18-20 minutes.
8. Remove from oven and let cool for 2-3 minutes before discarding.

Conclusion

Hope you liked all the recipes. These recipes are especially for Paleo and veg diet lovers who want to follow a Pagan diet schedule. Recipes include vegan meals and also desserts for vegetarians. Try these delicious meals at home and appreciate. Good luck!

Lightning Source UK Ltd.
Milton Keynes UK
UKHW020744170521
383853UK00005B/40